SHARKS

CONTENTS

Terror of the Deep? 5

Older than Dinosaurs 6

The Shark's Closest Relatives 7

Staying Afloat 8

When This Tooth You Have 10

Taking a Breath 11

Shark Senses 12

Where Are They? 14

The Great White Shark. 16

Three Threats 17

Water Babies. 18

FOLDOUT: Shark Body 19

Motherly Comforts. 23

Shark Junk Food. 24

Hammers and Bonnets 25

Gentle Giants 26

Speedy Swimmers 28

Six Common Sharks 30

Six Strange Sharks. 32

Shark Attacks 34

Amazing Shark Facts. 36

Glossary 37

Index. 38

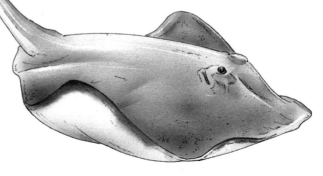

TERROR OF THE DEEP?

You may believe that sharks are large, silent, and deadly hunters. This is how sharks are often portrayed in the movies. Although sharks live in all the world's oceans, only half of the 250 species are larger than three feet and only a few types of sharks are dangerous. As we learn more about their fascinating habits and abilities, we will also learn to respect and admire these graceful creatures.

A Sailor's Nightmare
Since the days of the earliest seafarers, sharks have been dreaded monsters of the sea.

OLDER THAN DINOSAURS

The first sharks patrolled the seas about 300 million years ago, 100 million years before dinosaurs appeared. Some shark **species** died out. Most of those that survived have changed very little in the last 200 million years. Sharks are such successful hunters and have so few enemies that they simply have not needed to change.

The Biggest Shark
A shark called megalodon lived in the world's oceans until about 50,000 years ago. You can imagine how big megalodon was by comparing the size of its jaw to the people pictured below.

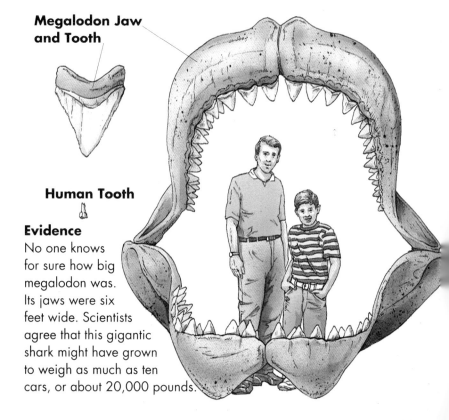

Megalodon Jaw and Tooth

Human Tooth

Evidence
No one knows for sure how big megalodon was. Its jaws were six feet wide. Scientists agree that this gigantic shark might have grown to weigh as much as ten cars, or about 20,000 pounds.

THE SHARK'S CLOSEST RELATIVES

Although they don't look like sharks, rays and skates, which swim by flapping their graceful "wings," are closely related to sharks. So are the six species of sawfish and about 48 species of guitarfish. While all true sharks have bony backbones, the skeletons of these fish are made of rubbery **cartilage** rather than bone.

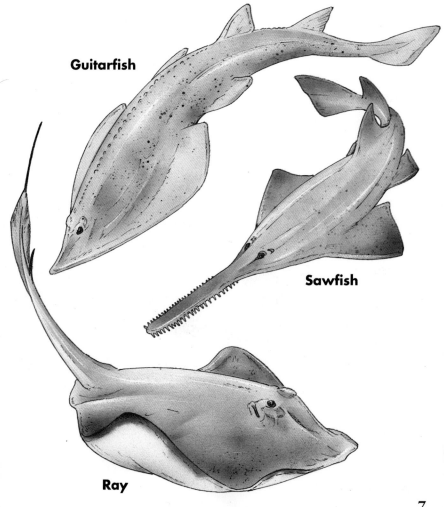

Guitarfish

Sawfish

Ray

STAYING AFLOAT

Because sharks are heavier than seawater, they would sink if they did not have special adaptations to stay afloat. A shark's liver contains oil, which is lighter than water and keeps the shark **buoyant**. Also, some sharks gulp air into their stomachs, which provides extra buoyancy.

Shark Skin
A shark's skin is covered with thousands of scales, called **denticles**, that point toward the tail. Because it is very rough when rubbed from back to front, shark skin was once used as sandpaper.

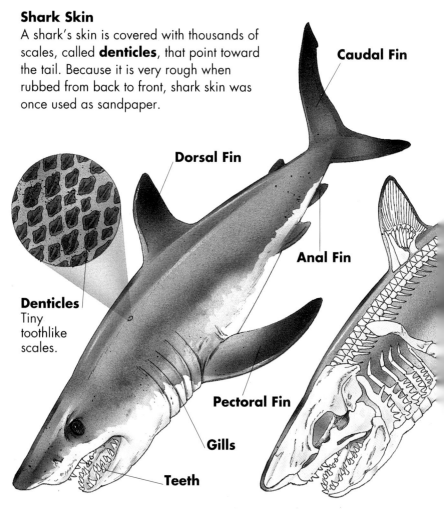

Caudal Fin

Dorsal Fin

Anal Fin

Denticles
Tiny toothlike scales.

Pectoral Fin

Gills

Teeth

A Shark's Body

Most sharks are **streamlined**. Their muscles, arranged in narrow zigzagging strips, squeeze in and out as sharks swim. This gives these sharks superb strength and speed in water and allows them to turn in tight circles.

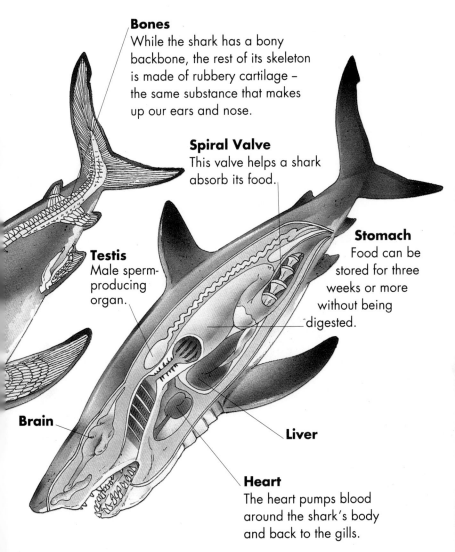

Bones
While the shark has a bony backbone, the rest of its skeleton is made of rubbery cartilage – the same substance that makes up our ears and nose.

Spiral Valve
This valve helps a shark absorb its food.

Stomach
Food can be stored for three weeks or more without being digested.

Testis
Male sperm-producing organ.

Brain

Liver

Heart
The heart pumps blood around the shark's body and back to the gills.

WHAT FINE TEETH YOU HAVE!

Sharks have several rows of teeth that come in different shapes and sizes, all designed for different jobs. When a front tooth falls out, the tooth behind moves forward to take its place. Sharks lose at least one tooth a week!

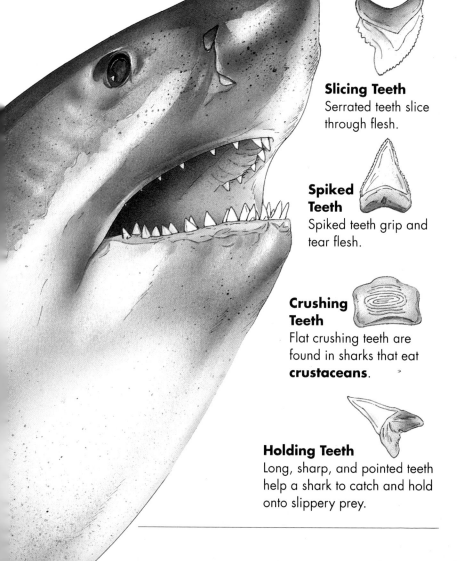

Slicing Teeth
Serrated teeth slice through flesh.

Spiked Teeth
Spiked teeth grip and tear flesh.

Crushing Teeth
Flat crushing teeth are found in sharks that eat **crustaceans**.

Holding Teeth
Long, sharp, and pointed teeth help a shark to catch and hold onto slippery prey.

TAKING A BREATH

Like all fish, sharks have gills that draw **oxygen** from the water and pass it into the **bloodstream**. Shark gills are open slits – usually five of them – without the folding flap that other fish have. Most sharks need to keep swimming to ensure they receive a sufficient flow of water over their gills. Some, however, can breathe while remaining still.

Gill Slits
Gill slits are like arches on a bridge: As a shark swims, water passes through the gill slits and into the gills.

Slow Swimmers.
Not all sharks swim fast. Some, like the wobbegong, rest on the seafloor. The spotted wobbegong moves from one rock pool to the next, searching for crabs and other crustaceans.

SHARK SENSES

A shark's senses are so acute that it can hear, smell, and detect movements of **prey** from very far away. A shark does not have ear flaps on the outside of its body. Its ears are inside its head on either side of the brain. Sharks can pick up sounds almost a mile away. And if an injured fish starts to bleed, some sharks can smell the blood more than 500 feet away!

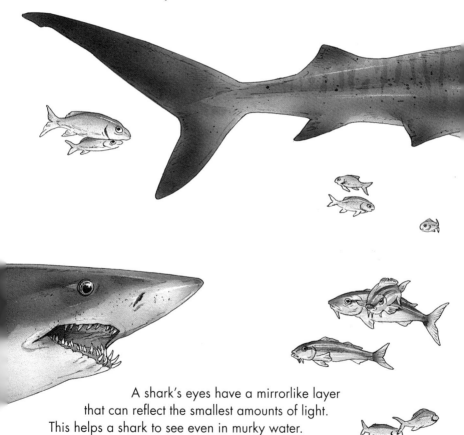

A shark's eyes have a mirrorlike layer
that can reflect the smallest amounts of light.
This helps a shark to see even in murky water.
However, sharks cannot see as well as humans can.

A shark's ears are inside its head, with tiny holes leading to the outside.

A shark relies more on its sense of smell than on its eyesight. A shark's nose and the front of its head are covered with tiny **pores** that can detect electrical impulses caused by the movements of other fish.

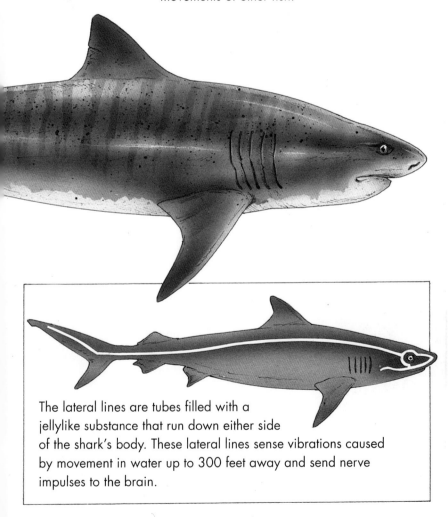

The lateral lines are tubes filled with a jellylike substance that run down either side of the shark's body. These lateral lines sense vibrations caused by movement in water up to 300 feet away and send nerve impulses to the brain.

WHERE ARE THEY?

There are 375 species of shark in the world's seas. Sharks come in a wide variety of shapes, sizes, and colors. Some sharks are wanderers, covering great distances, while others inhabit their own small territories. Most sharks are found in warm water. Although few sharks live in cold water, the great white shark has been found in the cold waters off the coast of Maine.

Tiger Shark
Ferocious by nature, the tiger shark prefers to swim in the upper 900 feet of the open sea. It occasionally moves inshore.

Goblin Shark
Goblin sharks have been on Earth for 70 million years. They live in the deepest and darkest seas. The long, rodlike projection on its snout helps it find food on the seafloor.

Blacktipped Reef Shark
This shark has a distinctive black **dorsal fin**. Like other shallow water sharks, it spends most of its life close to land, in water less than 600 feet deep.

Blue Shark
This shark is a midwater dweller. It rarely ventures near either the surface or the seafloor.

THE GREAT WHITE SHARK

The great white shark is the most dangerous
of all sharks. In size, it is as long as a bus.
Great whites are found in cool-to-warm
waters. Their favorite prey is seal.
They usually launch surprise attacks,
first wounding their victims, then waiting
for them to weaken before
returning to finish the meal.
Great white sharks will
attack people in shallow
water and drag them
out to sea.

Great White Shark
This shark will eat almost anything –
smaller sharks, fish, penguins, or
even people.

THREE THREATS

Several species of shark have attacked people. Along with the great white shark, tiger sharks and bull sharks are also dangerous. Bull sharks hunt in tropical seas and have been known to swim up freshwater rivers and even into lakes. However, there is a greater chance of being struck by lightning than there is of being attacked by a shark.

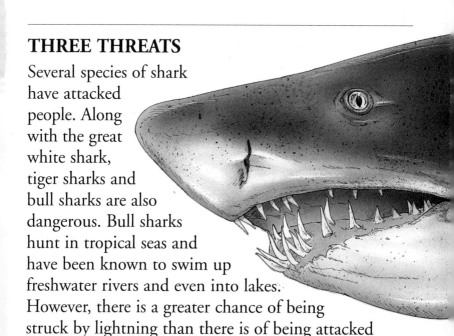

Mysteriously, sharks sometimes gather in large packs. Some of the biggest shark gatherings occur off the coastline of Central America.

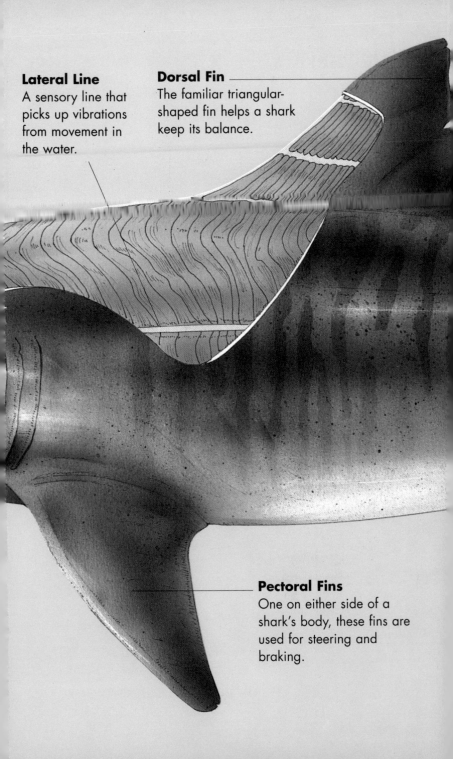

Lateral Line
A sensory line that picks up vibrations from movement in the water.

Dorsal Fin
The familiar triangular-shaped fin helps a shark keep its balance.

Pectoral Fins
One on either side of a shark's body, these fins are used for steering and braking.

SHARK BODY

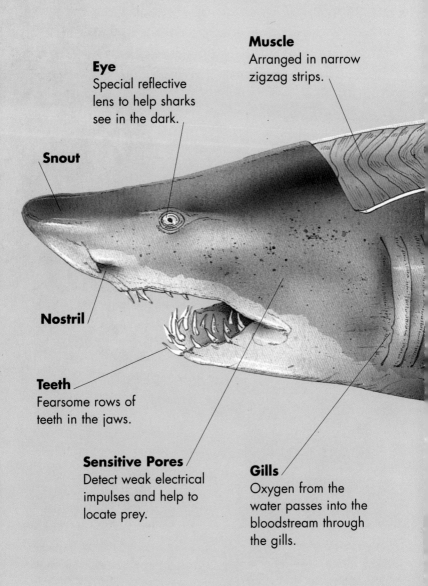

Eye
Special reflective lens to help sharks see in the dark.

Muscle
Arranged in narrow zigzag strips.

Snout

Nostril

Teeth
Fearsome rows of teeth in the jaws.

Sensitive Pores
Detect weak electrical impulses and help to locate prey.

Gills
Oxygen from the water passes into the bloodstream through the gills.

WATER BABIES

When mating, a male shark grasps its partner with its teeth, sometimes causing cuts and gashes. These usually heal up very quickly. At birth, sharks are strong enough to look after themselves. Sharks have three different methods of reproducing.

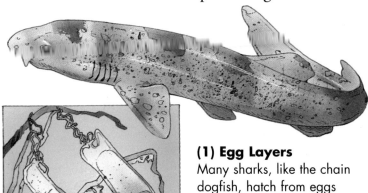

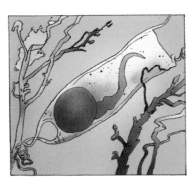

(1) Egg Layers
Many sharks, like the chain dogfish, hatch from eggs which are laid by the mother. The eggs are protected by a tough, leathery casing.

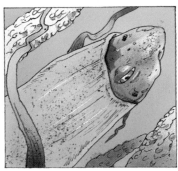

A shark develops inside each egg with its own food supply inside the sac. As the embryo grows, the egg-sac shrinks. This takes about nine months.

Then the baby shark searches for the weakest point in the egg case and forces its way out to freedom – a perfect miniature adult shark.

SHARK JUNK FOOD

Meat-eating sharks are known to have huge and varied appetites. Although sharks prefer fish, shellfish, and other marine life, sharks often swim behind boats and eat whatever is thrown overboard. This complete "menu" was found inside a gray shark, nearly fourteen feet in length, caught in Australian waters.

Menu

Starters

1 piece of packaging

1 metal scraper

Main course

8 legs of lamb

Half a ham

300 pounds of horse meat

Dessert

head and forelegs of a bulldog

hind-quarters of a pig

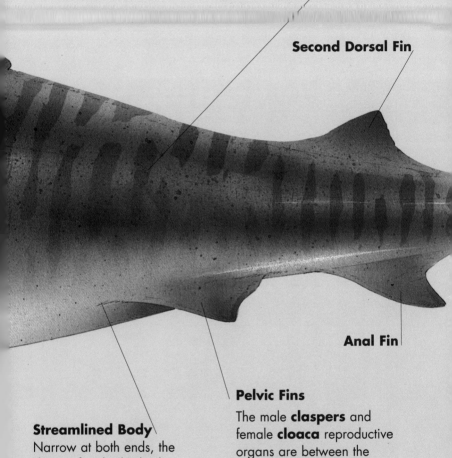

Skin

A shark's skin is rough because it is covered with tiny denticles. These small, hard scales have the same structure as a shark's teeth and are unique to sharks and rays. The shape of the denticles helps to identify some species of shark.

Second Dorsal Fin

Anal Fin

Pelvic Fins

The male **claspers** and female **cloaca** reproductive organs are between the pelvic fins. These fins also act as stabilizers to keep the shark from rolling as it swims.

Streamlined Body

Narrow at both ends, the shape of a shark's body helps it swim quickly.

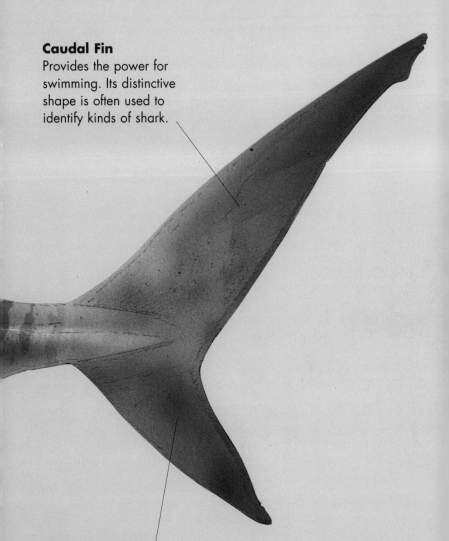

Caudal Fin
Provides the power for
swimming. Its distinctive
shape is often used to
identify kinds of shark.

Asymmetric Tail
A shark swims by moving its
tail from side to side. The
upper lobe of a shark's tail
is larger than the lower one.
This helps the shark to move
up and down as well as
forward through the water.
The asymmetric tail helps to
compensate for the fact that
sharks are heavier than water.

MOTHERLY COMFORTS

Most sharks give birth to live young instead of laying eggs outside the mother's body. Baby sharks develop inside a yolky egg in the womb. The embryos hatch and continue to develop until they are ready to be born as live baby sharks.

(2) Born in Water
When sharks are born, they are ready to eat solid food.

(3) Internal Egg Developers
Blue, lemon, and bull sharks grow in an egg inside their mother. The unborn shark pup is fed through a placenta, like humans and other mammals. Pregnant sharks will swim into the calm shallow waters of coastal lagoons to give birth.

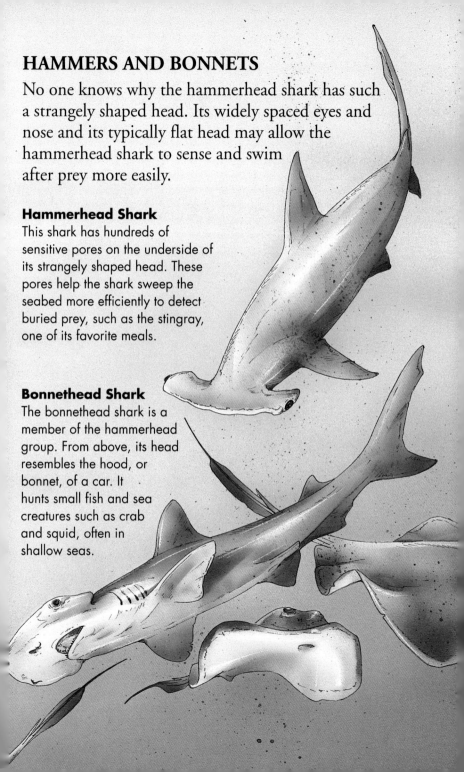

HAMMERS AND BONNETS

No one knows why the hammerhead shark has such a strangely shaped head. Its widely spaced eyes and nose and its typically flat head may allow the hammerhead shark to sense and swim after prey more easily.

Hammerhead Shark

This shark has hundreds of sensitive pores on the underside of its strangely shaped head. These pores help the shark sweep the seabed more efficiently to detect buried prey, such as the stingray, one of its favorite meals.

Bonnethead Shark

The bonnethead shark is a member of the hammerhead group. From above, its head resembles the hood, or bonnet, of a car. It hunts small fish and sea creatures such as crab and squid, often in shallow seas.

GENTLE GIANTS

The largest fish in the sea are the mighty whale shark and the basking shark. Neither of these giants is a threat to people. Instead of teeth, both have special filters in their mouths that strain tiny animals, called **zooplankton**, from the water.

The whale shark

This shark feeds during the day in deep, warm tropical oceans. It grows to about forty feet and can weigh more than twenty tons.

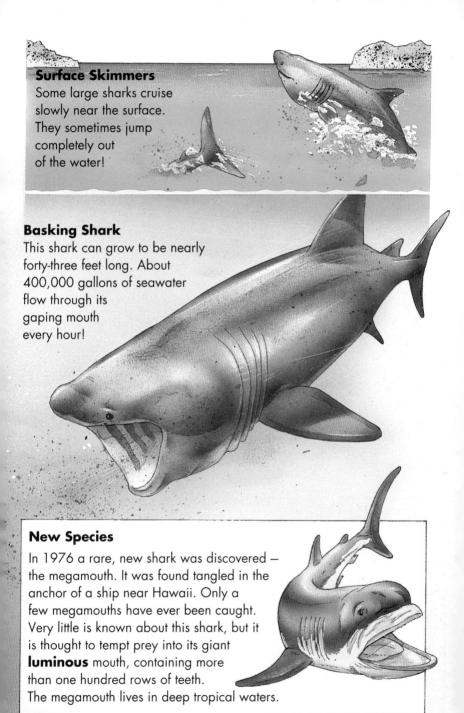

Surface Skimmers

Some large sharks cruise slowly near the surface. They sometimes jump completely out of the water!

Basking Shark

This shark can grow to be nearly forty-three feet long. About 400,000 gallons of seawater flow through its gaping mouth every hour!

New Species

In 1976 a rare, new shark was discovered — the megamouth. It was found tangled in the anchor of a ship near Hawaii. Only a few megamouths have ever been caught. Very little is known about this shark, but it is thought to tempt prey into its giant **luminous** mouth, containing more than one hundred rows of teeth.

The megamouth lives in deep tropical waters.

SPEEDY SWIMMERS

Sharks are specially designed for fast swimming. The only thing sharks cannot do, which most bony fish can, is swim backward.

Streamlining

A shark's streamlined shape makes it very agile and enables it to turn quickly. Also, its fins curve slightly toward its tail, helping the shark swim faster.

Fins for Lifting
The **pectoral fins** act like an airplane's wings to help create "lift" and move the shark up or down.

Thresher Shark
This shark's spine extends into the tail, giving it extra strength. The thresher shark's tail is actually longer than the rest of its body!

A Rudder

A shark's tail sweeps from side to side like a **rudder**, pushing the shark through the sea.

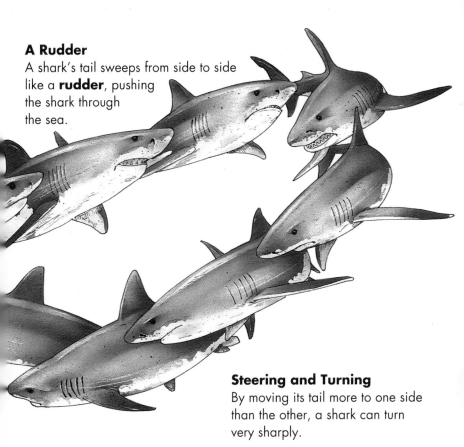

Steering and Turning

By moving its tail more to one side than the other, a shark can turn very sharply.

Shark Tails

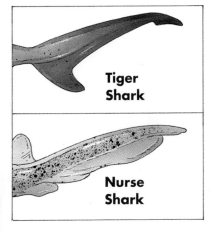

Tiger Shark

Nurse Shark

Great White Shark

Cookiecutter Shark

SIX COMMON SHARKS

Mako Shark
This agile shark's high speed helps
it catch tuna and mackerel, its
favorite foods. It swims
near the surface and
sometimes attacks boats.

Oceanic Whitetip
A tuna may mistake the white tips
of this shark's fins for small fish.
When the tuna approaches, it
finds itself lured into the shark's
trap and eaten.

Lemon Shark
A young lemon shark can
be aggressive towards
divers, but the adult lemon
shark is extremely shy. A
lemon shark eats fish that
live on the seafloor.

Sand Tiger Shark
This shark's needle-sharp teeth
make it look fierce, but it is not
very dangerous. In Australia it is
called the gray nurse shark. It eats
fish, smaller sharks, crabs, and
lobsters.

Leopard Shark
This striking, black-spotted shark
feeds mainly on clams. Common
along the Pacific coast of North
America, it is harmless to people.

Nurse Shark
This shark usually spends the day
on the seafloor in shallow water.
It sometimes attacks swimmers.
At night it searches
for crabs or small fish.

SIX STRANGE SHARKS

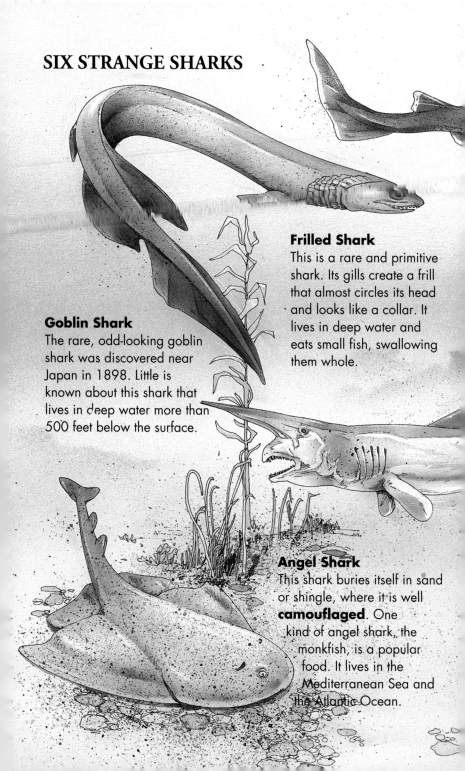

Frilled Shark
This is a rare and primitive shark. Its gills create a frill that almost circles its head and looks like a collar. It lives in deep water and eats small fish, swallowing them whole.

Goblin Shark
The rare, odd-looking goblin shark was discovered near Japan in 1898. Little is known about this shark that lives in deep water more than 500 feet below the surface.

Angel Shark
This shark buries itself in sand or shingle, where it is well **camouflaged**. One kind of angel shark, the monkfish, is a popular food. It lives in the Mediterranean Sea and the Atlantic Ocean.

Cookiecutter Shark

This small shark has strong jaws and razor-sharp teeth that take cookie-shaped bites out of its prey – seals, whales, and dolphins. The cookiecutter shark is sometimes called the cigar shark. It is very hard to catch because it can bite its way out of nets.

Spined Pygmy Shark

The smallest shark can fit in the palm of a hand. It is also the only one with a spine on its dorsal fin.

Wobbegong

This shark has a ragged strip of skin that hangs over its mouth and looks like seaweed. When a creature investigates this fringe the wobbegong strikes.

SHARK ATTACKS

Shark attacks on humans are nearly always caused by divers annoying the sharks or by the sharks mistaking swimmers or surfers for their usual prey. Researchers have tried many safeguards against attack, such as special diving suits and protective cages.

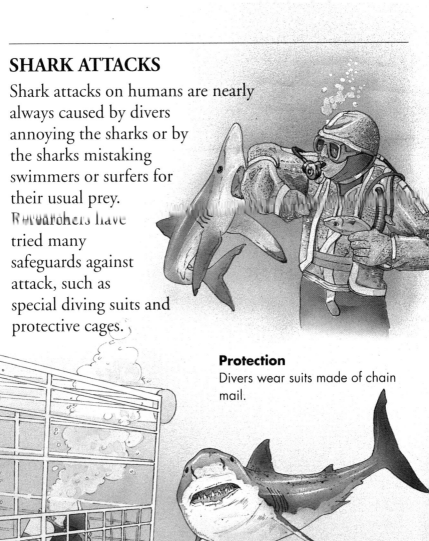

Protection
Divers wear suits made of chain mail.

Shark Cages
Divers use shark cages to protect themselves when studying sharks at close range. Movies of sharks are often photographed from shark cages.

Seal   **Turtle**   **Surfer**

Outlines
To a shark, the outline of a
person paddling on a surfboard
probably looks very similar to the
outline of a seal or turtle.

People kill a staggering
100 million sharks every year.
Sharks cannot survive such a high rate of slaughter,
especially because some larger species do not breed until
they are eighteen years old. Luckily, some countries are
now actively trying to protect certain species.

Killed for Food and Sport
Many harmless sharks are
killed in nets meant to protect
beaches from the dangerous
species.

AMAZING SHARK FACTS

Thresher Shark

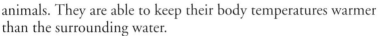

● **River Sharks** The Ganges and bull sharks are the only ones who leave the sea and swim into freshwater rivers.

● **Warm-blooded Sharks** Thresher sharks, great whites and tunas are warm-blooded animals. They are able to keep their body temperatures warmer than the surrounding water.

● **Cookiecutter Sharks** These sharks swim about twenty-five miles each day, moving up from the depths of the ocean to feed near the surface.

● **Great White Shark** It is thought that some great white sharks can live for a hundred years.

● **Spiny Dogfish** The spiny dogfish may be the most common shark in the world. Between 1904 and 1905, 27 million were caught off the U.S. coast alone. These sharks range widely through the world's oceans.

● **Horn Shark** Sharks' eggs come in an assortment of shapes and sizes. One of the strangest is the egg of the horn shark, which has its own screwthread, enabling the mother shark to fasten the egg securely in a rocky crack.

● **Sawfish** The sawfish slashes through schools of fish, stunning and stabbing them with the lateral teeth on either side of its 6-foot long upper jaw.

● **Spinner Shark** The spinner shark has a unique way of eating. It does not chase fish. Instead, this shark confuses small fish by leaping and spinning. Then the shark attacks its prey.

Sawfish

GLOSSARY

Bloodstream Blood flowing through the circulatory system of an animal.

Buoyant Able to float, or rise to the surface of water.

Camouflage An animal's coloring that blends in with the surroundings, enabling it to hide from its enemies.

Claspers Male reproductive organs that are inserted into the female and pump sperm.

Cartilage The tough, flexible tissue that forms part of the skeleton. Human ears and noses are made of cartilage.

Chain mail diving suit A flexible armor of interlocking metal loops, worn to protect divers from shark bites.

Cloaca The female reproductive opening and vent for waste disposal.

Crustacean An animal with a hard outer shell like shrimp, crabs, and lobsters.

Denticles The toothlike covering that gives a shark's skin its rough feel.

Dorsal fin The fin on a shark's back that is visible above the water when a shark is swimming close to the surface.

Luminous An object that glows in the dark.

Oxygen A gas found in air and water that is essential to life.

Pectoral fins The fins on either side of a fish's body that help the animal to change direction as it swims.

Pores Tiny openings that allow liquid or air to pass through the skin and into the body.

Prey Animals that are eaten by other animals.

Rudder A steering device.

Species A group of animals or plants that are alike in some ways.

Streamlined Having a shape that allows quick and easy movement through water or air.

Zooplankton Tiny floating creatures that live in the ocean and are eaten by much larger animals.

INDEX   *(Entries in **bold** refer to an illustration)*

A
pages
anal fin 8, 21
angel shark 32

B
basking shark 26, 27
blacktipped reef shark . . . 15
blue shark 15, 23
bonnethead shark 25
bull shark 17, 23, 36

C
cartilage 7, 9, 37
caudal fin 8, 22
chain dogfish 18
cookiecutter shark 29, 33, 36
crab 11, 25, 31
crustacean 10, 11, 37

D
dangerous 5, 17
denticles 8, 21, 37
dinosaur 6
dolphin 33
dorsal fin . . . 8, 15, 20, 33, 37

E
ear 12, 13
eye 12, 13, 19

F
fin 21, 22, 28
fish 7, 11, 12, 13, 16,
. . . . 25, 26, 28, 30, 31, 32
frilled shark 32

G
pages
Ganges shark 36
gills 8, 9, 11, 19, 32
goblin shark 14, 32
great white shark . 14, 16, 17,
19, 35
guitarfish 7

H
hammerhead shark 25
horn shark 36

J
jaw 6, 19, 33

L
lateral line 13
lemon shark 23, 30
leopard shark 31
luminous 27, 37

M
mackerel 30
mako shark 30
megalodon 6
megamouth 27
monkfish 32

N
nose 13, 25
nurse shark 29, 31

O
oceanic whitetip 30
oil 8
oxygen 11, 19, 37